Number Puzzles and Games

D1318561

Written by **Kerrie Baldwin**

Illustrations by **Nan Brooks**

An imprint of Sterling Children's Books

This book belongs to

_____

FLASH KIDS, STERLING, and the distinctive Sterling logo are registered trademarks of
Sterling Publishing Co., Inc.

Published by Sterling Publishing Co., Inc.
387 Park Avenue South, New York, NY 10016
Text and illustrations © 2006 by Flash Kids
Distributed in Canada by Sterling Publishing
c/o Canadian Manda Group, 165 Dufferin Street
Toronto, Ontario, Canada M6K 3H6
Distributed in the United Kingdom by GMC Distribution Services
Castle Place, 166 High Street, Lewes, East Sussex, England BN7 1XU
Distributed in Australia by Capricorn Link (Australia) Pty. Ltd.
P.O. Box 704, Windsor, NSW 2756, Australia

Sterling ISBN 978-1-4114-3464-6

Manufactured in Canada

Lot #:
10 12 14 13 11 9
04/13

For information about custom editions, special sales, premium and
corporate purchases, please contact Sterling Special Sales
Department at 800-805-5489 or specialsales@sterlingpublishing.com.

Cover design and production by Mada Design, Inc.

Dear Parent,

Learning to count is an important step for every child. *Number Puzzles and Games* is a fun way to help your child identify numbers and count to ten and beyond. The book includes counting activities, dot-to-dots, hidden pictures, and simple mazes. To get the most from *Number Puzzles and Games*, follow these simple steps:

- Find a comfortable place where you and your child can work quietly.
- Help your child read the simple directions at the top of each activity.
- Encourage your child to go at his or her own pace. Offer lots of praise and support.
- Let your child reward his or her work with the included stickers.
- Most of all, remember that learning should be fun! Take time to color the pictures, talk about the activities, and enjoy this special time spent together.

Which number is next?

1 2 3 4 ___

Hint: Count the roosters.

Who wakes up the farm?

Connect the dots from 1 to 5.

Color the picture.

Find the hidden picture.

Color the spaces that show 1 dot.

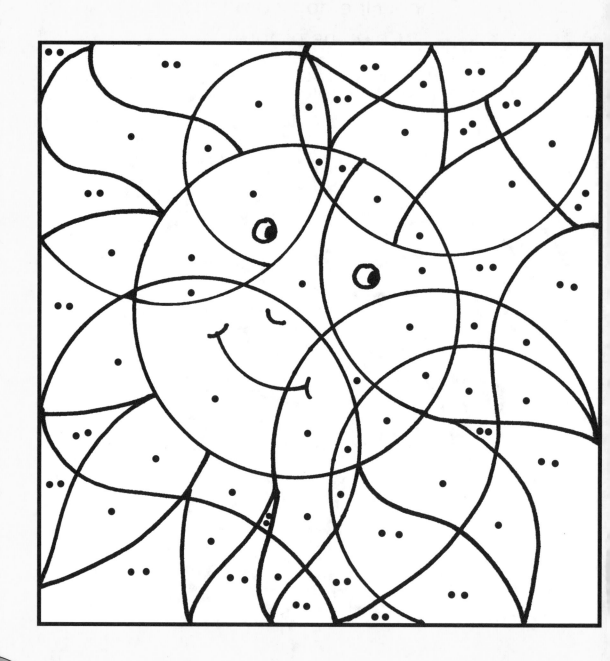

Help the early bird get the worm.

Follow the path that shows the numbers in order.

Which number is next?

1 2 3 4 5 6 ___

Hint: Count the eggs.

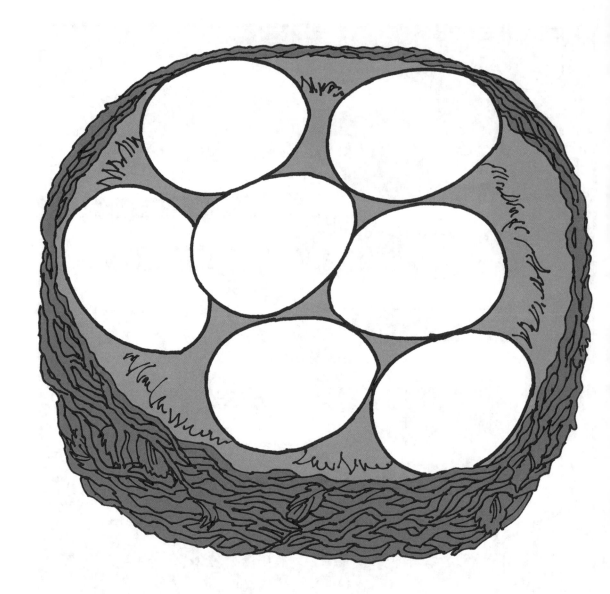

Who is in the egg?

Connect the dots from 1 to 7.

Color the picture.

Find the hidden picture.

Color the spaces that show 2 dots.

Help the farmer catch the egg.

Follow the path that shows the numbers in order.

Which number is next?

1 2 3 4 5 6 7 8 __

Hint: Count the bottles of milk.

Where does milk come from?

Connect the dots from 1 to 10.
Color the picture.

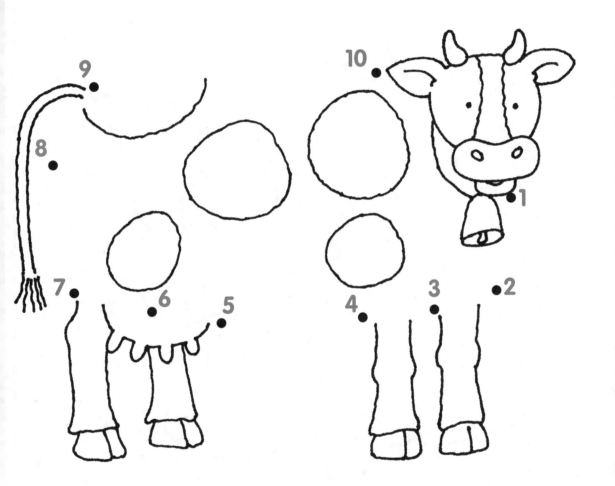

Find the hidden picture.

Color the spaces that show 3 dots.

Help the farmer milk the last cow.

Follow the path that shows the numbers in order.

Which number is missing?

1 2 3 __ 5 6 7 8

Hint: Count the oranges.

What is for breakfast?

Connect the dots from 1 to 12.

Color the picture.

Find the hidden picture.

Color the spaces that show 4 dots.

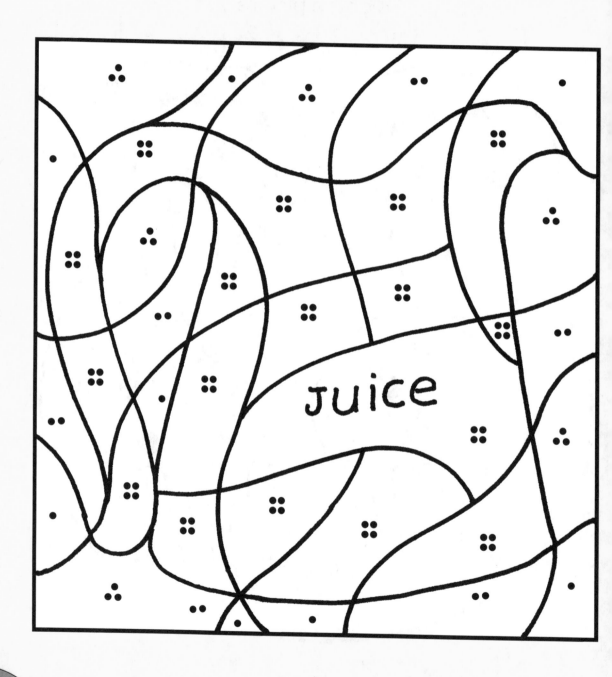

Oh, no! The sausage rolled across the floor.

Help the farmer find it. Follow the path that shows the numbers in order.

Which number is missing?

1 2 __ 4 5 6 7 8 9

Hint: Count the lambs.

Who grows wool?

Connect the dots from 1 to 10.

Color the picture.

Find the hidden picture.

Color the spaces that show 5 dots.

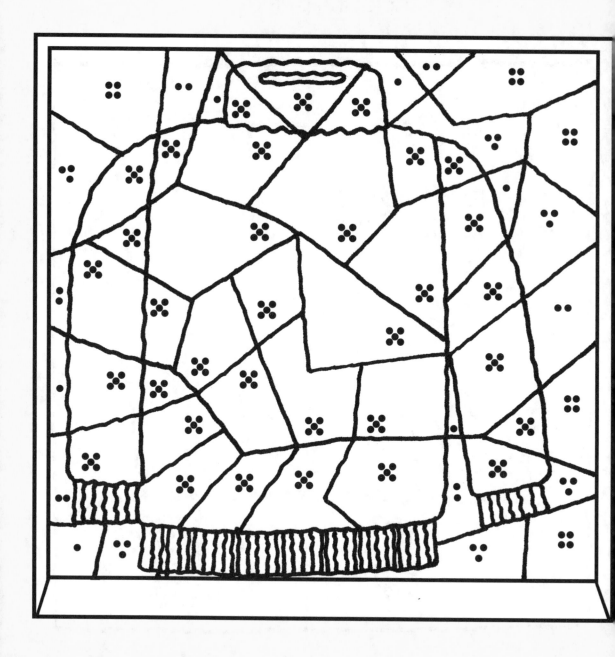

Help the sheep eat the grass.

Follow the path that shows the numbers in order.

Which number is next?

1 2 3 4 5 6 7 8 9 10 __

Hint: Count the ears of corn.

Who eats the corn?

Connect the dots from 1 to 12.

Color the picture.

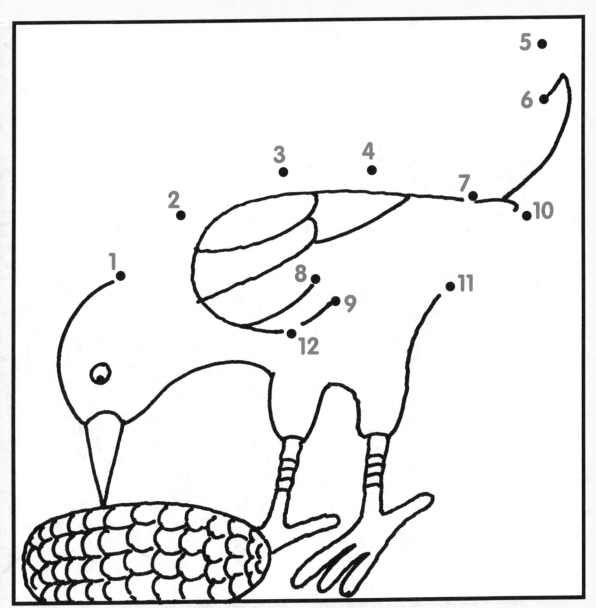

Find the hidden picture.

Color the spaces that have 6 dots.

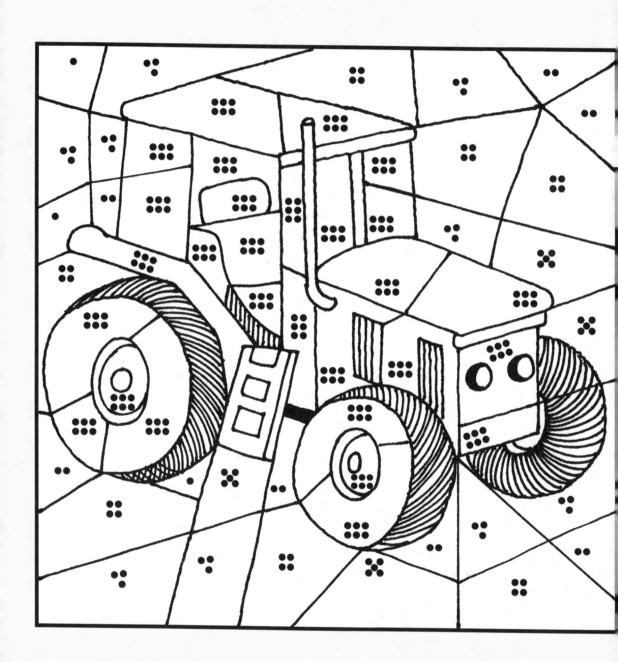

Help bring the corn to the barn.

Follow the path that shows the numbers in order.

Which number is missing?

1 2 3 4 5 6 7 8 9 ___ 11 12 13 14

Hint: Count the horseshoes.

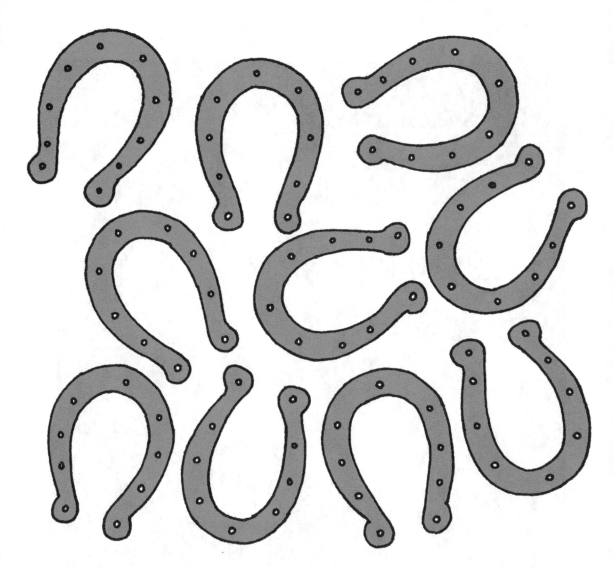

Which animal is fun to ride?

Connect the dots from 1 to 10.
Color the picture.

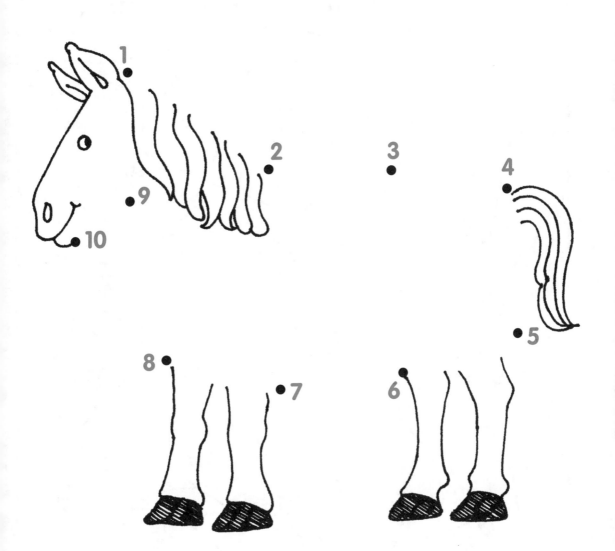

Find the hidden picture.

Color the spaces that have 7 dots.

Ride the horse back to the stable.

Follow the path that shows the numbers in order.

Which number is next?

1 2 3 4 5 6 7 __

Hint: Count the pigs.

Who rolls in the mud?

Connect the dots from 1 to 12.

Color the picture.

Find the hidden picture.
Color the spaces that have 8 dots.

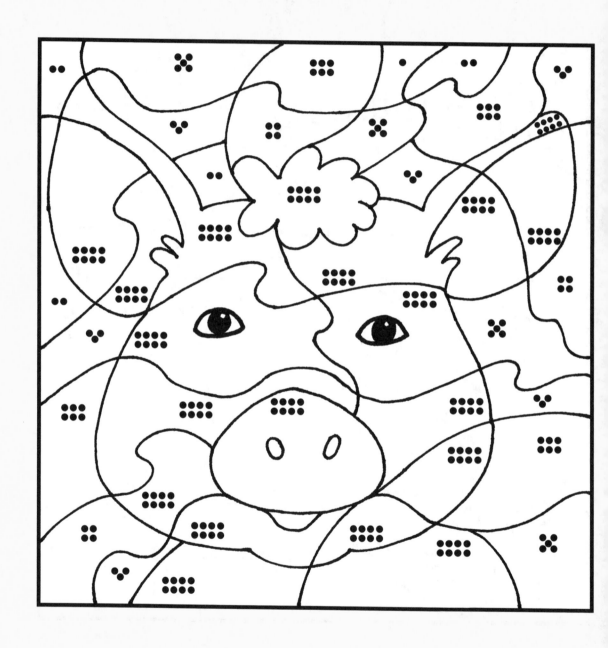

Feed the pigs.

Follow the path that shows the numbers in order.

Which number is missing?

1 2 3 4 __ 6 7 8 9 10

Hint: Count the frogs.

What is for lunch?

Connect the dots from 1 to 14.
Color the picture.

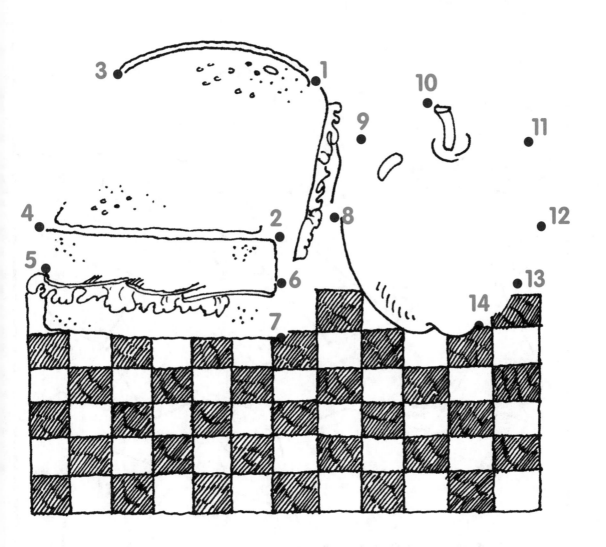

Find the hidden picture.

Color the spaces that have 9 dots.

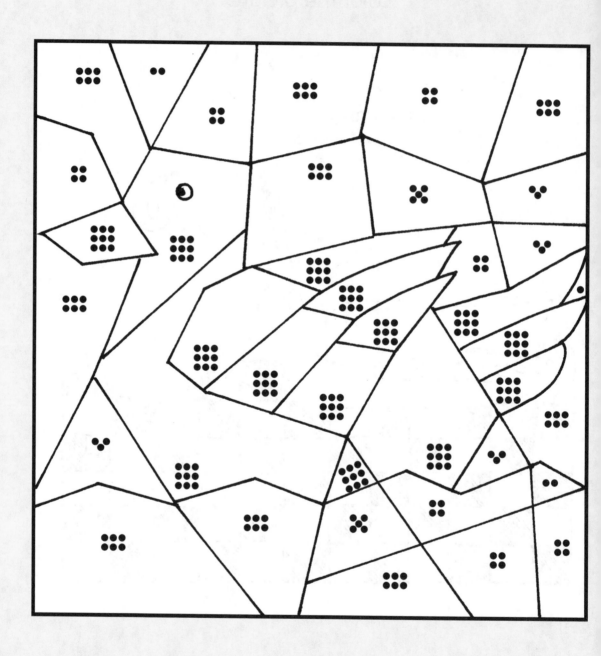

Help the duck find the crumbs.

Follow the path that shows the numbers in order.

Which number is next?

1 2 3 4 5 6 7 8 9 10 11 12 13 ___

Hint: Count the strawberries.

What is the biggest fruit on the farm?

Connect the dots from 1 to 10.

Color the picture.

Find the hidden picture.

Color the spaces that have 10 dots.

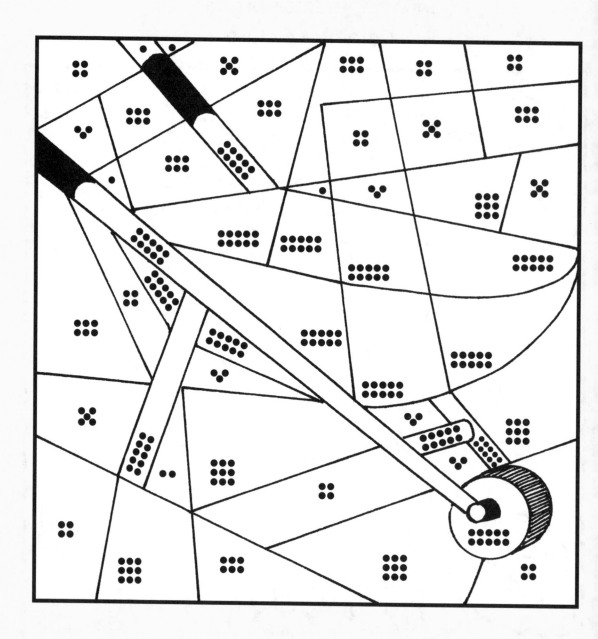

Bring the strawberries to the house.

Follow the path that shows the numbers in order.

Which number is missing?

1 2 3 4 5 __ 7 8 9 10 11

Hint: Count the bales of hay.

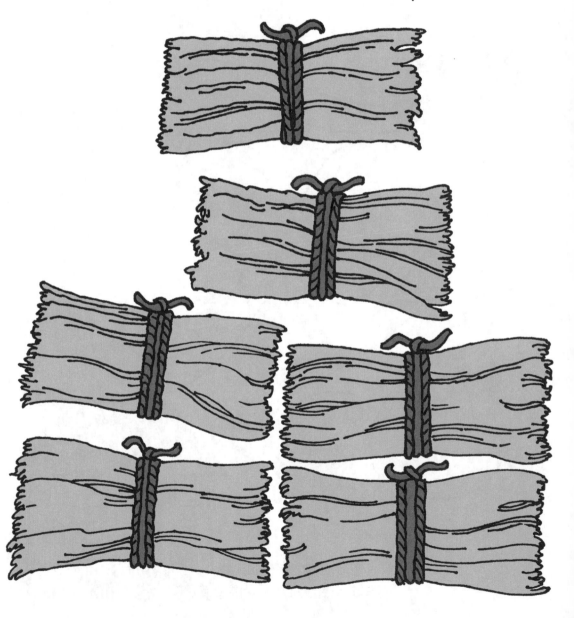

Who eats the hay?

Connect the dots from 1 to 15.
Color the picture.

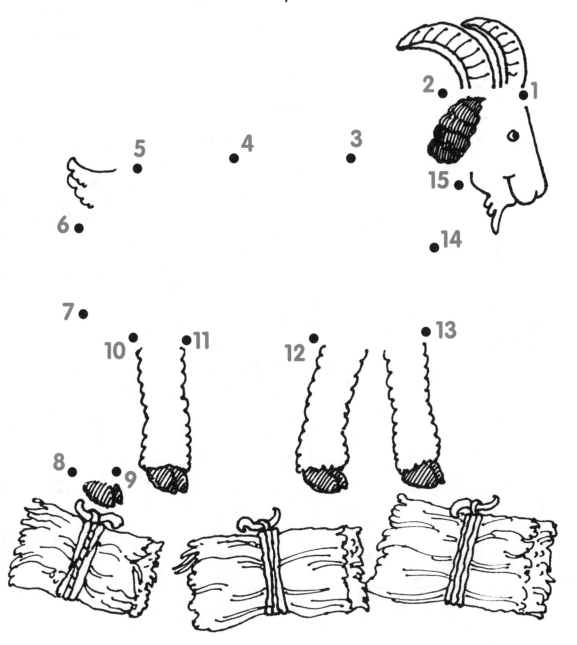

Find the hidden picture.

Color the spaces that have 5 dots.

Bring the hay to the horse.

Follow the path that shows the numbers in order.

Which number is next?

1 2 3 4 5 6 7 8 ___

Hint: Count the pickets on the fence.

What fixes the fence?

Connect the numbers from 1 to 12.
Color the picture.

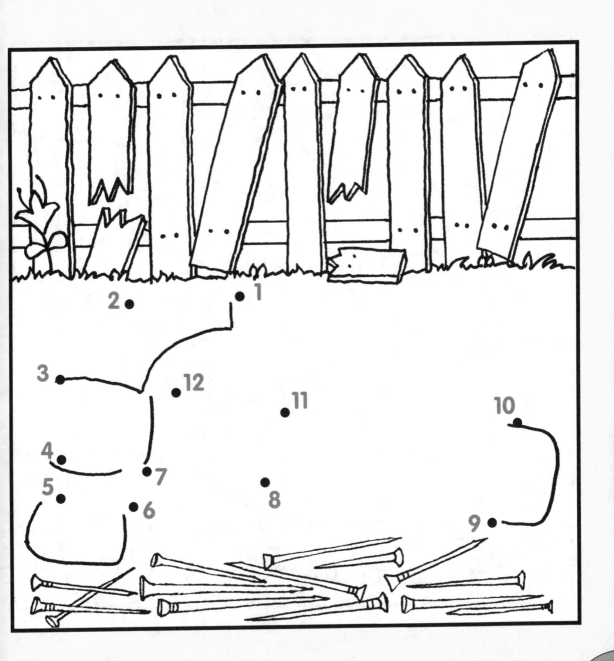

Find the hidden picture.

Color the spaces that have 7 dots.

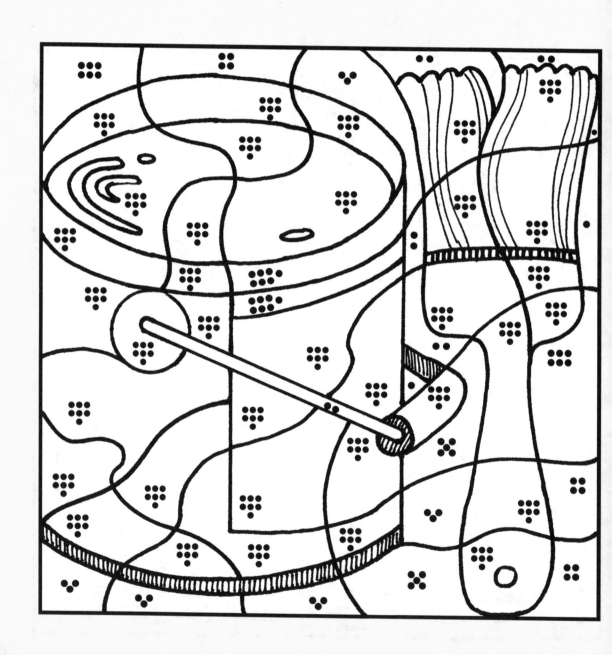

Help the farmer find the missing nail.

Follow the path that shows the numbers in order.

51

Which number is missing?

1 2 3 4 5 6 7 8 9 10 11 ___ 13 14 15

Hint: Count the raindrops.

Who likes to get wet?

Connect the dots from 1 to 10.

Color the picture.

Find the hidden picture.

Color the spaces that have 3 dots.

Bring the water
back to the house.

Follow the path that shows the numbers in order.

Which number is next?

1 2 3 4 5 6 7 8 __

Hint: Count the carrots.

What is for dinner?

Connect the dots from 1 to 13.

Color the picture.

Find the hidden picture.

Color the spaces that have 8 dots.

Bring your plate to the sink.

Follow the path that shows the numbers in order.

Which number is missing?

1 2 __ 4 5 6 7 8 9 10

Hint: Count the soap bubbles in the air.

Where do you take a bath?

Count the dots from 1 to 15.

Color the picture.

Find the hidden picture.

Color the spaces that have 10 dots.

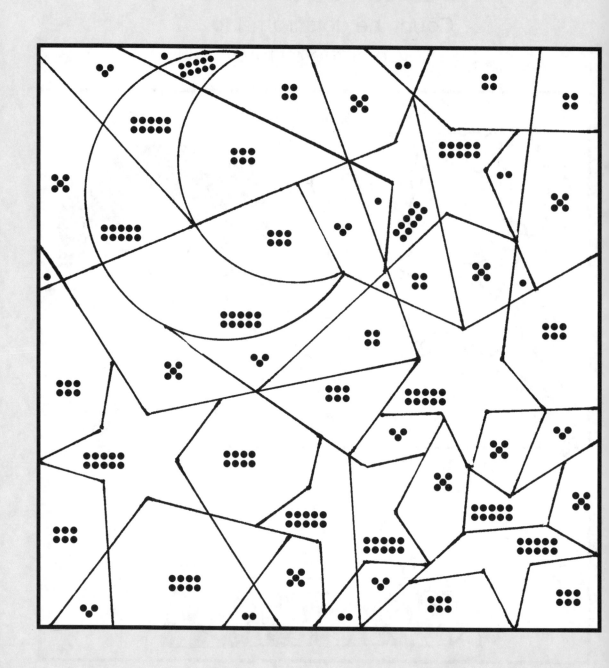

What a long day!

Find your way to bed. Follow the path that shows the numbers in order.

_____,
(Name)

you did a great job!

Learning numbers was as easy as 1, 2, 3!